IN OTHER WORDS

AN ILLUSTRATED MISCELLANY OF THE WORLD'S MOST INTRIGUING WORDS AND PHRASES

CHRISTOPHER J. MOORE

BLOOMSBURY PUBLISHING

NEW YORK · LONDON · OXFORD · NEW DELHI · SYDNEY

BLOOMSBURY PUBLISHING
Bloomsbury Publishing Inc.
1385 Broadway, New York, NY 10018, USA

BLOOMSBURY, BLOOMSBURY PUBLISHING, and the Diana logo are
trademarks of Bloomsbury Publishing Plc

Some of the text from this book appeared in a previous edition of *In Other Words*
(Bloomsbury 2004)
Published in Great Britain by Elwin Street Productions Limited in 2017
This edition published in the United States by Bloomsbury Publishing in 2019

Text by Christopher J. Moore
Illustrations by Lan Truong
Foreword by Simon Winchester

Bloomsbury Publishing Plc does not have any control over, or responsibility for, any
third-party websites referred to or in this book. All internet addresses given in this
book were correct at the time of going to press. The author and publisher regret any
inconvenience caused if addresses have changed or sites have ceased to exist, but can
accept no responsibility for any such changes.

ISBN: HB: 978-1-63557-403-6

Library of Congress Cataloging-in-Publication Data is available

2 4 6 8 10 9 7 5 3 1

Printed in China

To find out more about our authors and books visit www.bloomsbury.com and
sign up for our newsletters.

Bloomsbury books may be purchased for business or promotional use. For
information on bulk purchases please contact Macmillan Corporate and
Premium Sales Department at specialmarkets@macmillan.com.

CONTENTS

PRONUNCIATION GUIDE

Words and phrases are shown as phonetically pronounced by an English speaker, with the stress shown in capitals. Where some compound words have two stresses, as in German, the first will be the stronger. Some specific vowels and consonants are indicated below.

j- is the French sound j-, a soft slurred *jay*.
dj- is the English sound j-, as in *jail*.
tch- is the sound ch-, as in *chatter*.
ch- or -ch is the sound ch, as in Scottish *loch*.
-onh is the nasal French sound *on*.
-anh is the nasal French sound *in*.
-o- is a short o, as in *hot*.
-oh- is a long o, as in *comb*.
-a- is a short a, as in *fat*.
-ay- is the long a, as in *fake*.
-ah is a long a, as in *far*.
-i is a short -i-, as in *dip*.
-ye- is a long -i-, as in *hide*.

FOREWORD

People who are not us speak, write, and do things that are alien and mysterious but that, when explained, often make an awful lot of sense; the moment you understand the words and phrases and the wonderful concepts that they frequently encapsulate, you have come some small way toward understanding the people who employ them. Which, it seems to me, is the prime benefit (aside from the serendipitous pleasures of browsing) of the delightful treasure house—literally thesaurus—of the linguistic marvels that follow.

I have always enjoyed the English tongue's singular oddities—try explaining to foreigners the subtleties of phrases such as "hair of the dog"—but, having lived in China for many years, I have long believed the East to be more richly endowed with untranslatable concepts than any other part of the world. Take the Chinese word *mianzi*. Having no other word to use, we call this "face," and it represents, very roughly, the inner dignity that is possessed by every human, which all others dealing with its possessor are duty bound to uphold. Shout an insult at a Chinese shopkeeper and you make him lose face, you threaten his *mianzi*, and you commit the most cardinal of sins.

Whenever I find myself drifting dreamily back to my beloved East, I find myself wondering how it can be that we speak a language that has no equivalent for the most delicious of all Japanese phrases: *mono-no-aware*, which means no less than appreciating the sadness of existence. You see the cherry blossoms on the trees in Kyoto in April and you love them, but you love them most of all because you appreciate that soon they will all be gone.

Mono-no-aware: a phrase that like all Japanese words has every syllable pronounced, which deserves never to be lost in translation and that serves as a reminder that the understanding of tongues other than our own offers us a chance to come to a better understanding of peoples other than ourselves—an understanding that can only be for the betterment of us all.

Simon Winchester

INTRODUCTION

It was Benjamin Lee Whorf, in *Language, Thought, and Reality,* who introduced the theory that language proceeds from and shapes our cultural life. Whorf's research into the speech of the Hopi Indians, whose language has no concept of tenses, started a wave of inquiry into the relationship between language and culture. Academics refer to this area of study as "sociolinguistics." What emerges is not only the universal phenomenon that certain languages have "no word for X"—for example, the Algonquin people have no word for time and there is no word for snow in Inuktitut (Eskimo)—but also, conversely, that languages and cultures have terms and ideas that are simply untranslatable.

No word for snow? The truth is, there are too many words, just as in English we have snowstorm, flurry, drift, bank, flake, and fall, not to mention slush. More annoyingly for northern Europeans, the southern Europeans cannot translate the incredibly simple word "berry." For the French, Spanish, and Italians, berries are generically just "fruit" (each with its own name), but for the Swedes, Norwegians, Germans, and British, a berry is a berry, and in each instance a blackberry, raspberry, strawberry, blueberry (bilberry), cloudberry, and so on. What is it about the southerners that they cannot see a berry family there? Isn't it obvious?

Well, maybe not, as the Japanese apparently have no word for "water." Or more precisely, *mizu,* the word for water, actually means "cold water" as opposed to *oyu,* "hot water." It's possible that, for the Japanese, hot and cold water must be so different that they cannot be grouped under the same word. You might just as well say, as Alice's Mad Hatter argued, that there is no resemblance between hot coffee and cold coffee. Come to think of it, maybe the Japanese are on to something.

But then, more bafflingly, the Japanese had to borrow a Western word for something seemingly unknown to them, and render it as *kissu.* As Glenn Grant asks, "I've always wondered what the Japanese did with their lips before adopting the loan-word *kissu.* I mean, what did they call it before? If they didn't have a word for it, does that mean they never did it?" We might just as well ask, to echo the Mad Hatter again, why the French insist on *embrasser* meaning "to kiss," when it quite plainly means "to embrace," while they use the word *baiser* to mean something considerably more intimate.

We all borrow words when it suits us to do so, when our own tongue has no equivalent; modern languages are like archaeological digs once we begin to explore where many of our words in daily use come from. Western mathematicians, for instance, had no idea of the concept of "zero" until Arab terminology gave it to them, along with *algebra* and *algorithm*.

In addition, we suppose that the most common experiences are the same as, and translatable between, different cultures, but this simply isn't so. Take the example of dreaming. What are we to make of the fact that languages such as Spanish and Italian have the same noun for sleep as for dream, while others, like French and English, differentiate between the two? Do some nations sleep differently from others? And what we mean by "dreaming" is plainly not the same as *aljerre* ("dream") in Aranda, an Aboriginal language of central Australia. For the native Australians, dreaming is a vital way of holding the world together. Bruce Chatwin writes, "aboriginal myths tell of the legendary totemic beings who wandered across the country in the Dreamtime . . . singing the world into existence." The belief is that, if the tribe's Keeper of the Dreaming fails to carry out his "dreaming" task of walking the songlines that put the world together, Earth as we know it will come to an end.

With unbridgeable gaps at such a basic level, how much more untranslatable are higher realizations attained through a lifetime's discipline. Oriental philosophy and spirituality are full of such terms; *nirvana*, *mantra*, and *yoga* being just a few.

Enjoy the selection of some of my favorite words and phrases gathered here. As well as entertaining you, I hope they open a window onto the diverse cultures and languages that our world can and should celebrate.

Christopher J. Moore

ASIA AND THE MIDDLE EAST

Westerners who have lived or worked in Asia and the Middle East are all too aware that the cultural differences from the West can be daunting, if not completely baffling at times. The differences are not only profound but ancient.

No conceptual difference could illustrate this more than the Eastern approach to time relationships. Chinese, for instance, has no tenses and lacks the simple linear approach to time found in Western languages. Temporal relations are treated as "aspects" or ways of juxtaposing things, which are much more subtle and alterable. Events are not lined up one by one through rigorously logical sequence but may be visualized, so to speak, simultaneously.

It is very clear when the holy book of a certain people, in this case the Koran, is alternatively known as "The Untranslatable" that we are entering a region with some interesting cultures and specific ways of

saying things. Arab oral traditions can perhaps be summed up by the following untranslatable word: *Halca* is an artistic genre so famed—and threatened—that it is now under UNESCO cultural protection. To describe *halca* simply as "storytelling" would do an injustice to this ancient Arab street tradition of improvised song, dance, and story where the audience gathers in a circle around the performers.

The hero story cycles of Middle Eastern culture belong in the same tradition as *alf layla wa layla*, more commonly known to Westerners as *One Thousand and One Nights* or *The Arabian Nights*. These stories owe their origins largely to the storytelling traditions of the Persian and Arab worlds. They are a valuable source of Middle Eastern social history across the medieval Islamic period. Of course, much of the subtleties of the language are lost in the translation, but the exotic and romantic imagery that remains is universal and inspirational.

HILM IL-'UTAAT KULLU FIRAAN

(Arabic) [HELM el-o-TAHT KUL-lu fi-rahn]

It can be translated as "the dream of cats is all about mice."
And the meaning? To have a one-track mind!

DAST U DEL BÃZ BUDAN

(Persian) [DAST oo DEL BOZ boo-DAN]

This phrase literally means "the opening of hand and heart." It describes the idea of being free with your money, not being stingy, and having a generosity toward others.

DENIZE DÜSEN YILANASARILIR

(Turkish) [den-i-ZEH dyoo-SHEN yi-lan-asa-ri-LIR]

A phrase that evokes imagery of the ocean, it literally translates as, "if you fall into the sea, hold onto a snake." This illustrates the understanding that you will accept help in any way, no matter what it looks like, if you are in a bad situation.

JEGAR

(Persian) [djeh-GAR]

Jegar, literally "liver," is a common term of endearment in Persian—and implies that you can't live without your sweetheart.

BAKSHEESH

(Arabic) [bak-SHEESH]

This word encompasses different kinds of giving of small amounts of money and acts as an informal welfare system. If you are wealthy, it is incumbent on you to share the wealth in small ways. This can be done in three main ways. The first is as a small reward or tip for a small service rendered. The second usually involves the granting of favors. Examples might include letting you into a historical site after hours, finding you a seat or a sleeper on a train that is "full," or speeding up some bureaucratic process. The last kind of *baksheesh* is alms-giving, an important social custom, and a tenet of Islam whereby the giver is made holy by the action.

GÖNÜL

(Turkish) [ger-NYOOL]

This word literally translates as "heart." But it is more than this, because you can also translate the Turkish words *yürek* and *kalp* as "heart." *Gönül* is something deeper. It belongs to your inner self and the energy that is within you. There is an element of the hearts of all people being united in your heart because you wish for their well-being.

TARAADIN

(Arabic) [tah-RAH-den]

Arabic has no word for "compromise" in the sense of reaching an arrangement via struggle and disagreement. But a much happier concept, *taraadin*, exists in Arabic. It implies a happy solution for everyone, an "I win, you win." It's a way of resolving a problem without anyone losing face.

SHIBUI

(Japanese) [shib-OO-ee]

Shibui describes an aesthetic that only time can reveal. As we become older and more marked by the riches of life's experience, we radiate with a beauty that stems from becoming fully ourselves. The term can be applied to almost anything—a person, a house, or even a piece of aged wood.

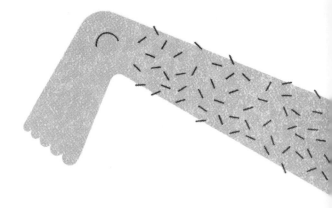

HIZA O MAJIERU

(Japanese) [hee-zah oh mah-djee-AIR-oo]

This phrase means "to have a talk." However, Japanese words are heavy with multiple meanings. This particular conversation's intimacy is conveyed by the literal meaning of this phrase, "to mingle knees with one another."

YOKO MESHI

(Japanese) [YO-ko MEH-shee]

As an untranslatable, this one ranks high on my list of favorites. I could not improve on the background given by commentator Boyé Lafayette de Mente about this beautiful word, *yoko meshi*. Taken literally, *meshi* means "boiled rice" and *yoko* means "horizontal," so combined you get "a meal eaten sideways."

This is how the Japanese define the peculiar stress induced by speaking a foreign language: yoko is a humorous reference to the fact that Japanese is normally written vertically, whereas most foreign languages are written horizontally. How do English-speakers describe the headache of communicating in an alien tongue? I don't think we can, at least not with as much ease.

DÌ ZHŌNG HǍI

(Mandarin) [DEE jong HIE]

"The sea in the middle of lands" (for instance, the Mediterranean) is a lovely image for someone who is bald. Mandarin also has other such metaphors for describing people's appearances; for instance, large women may be called *you tong*, "pillar box," or even *wan dun ju lun*, "ten-thousand-ton ocean-going ship."

FENG SHUI

(Mandarin) [feng shoo-AY]

Literally "wind water," this is the study and practice of arranging your life to align with surrounding nature, in particular the location and furnishing of your house. Now so fashionable in the West, it barely needs more comment.

WABI-SABI

(Japanese) [WAB-ee-SAB-ee]

Meaning something like "tranquil," *wabi* is one of the most important words in the extensive aesthetic vocabulary of Japanese. Unless something has *wabi*, it simply isn't Japanese. The first people involved with *wabi-sabi*, that is, the aesthetic system that places *wabi* at its center, were Zen Buddhists—tea masters, priests, and monks, who emphasized a direct, intuitive insight into transcendental truth. Therefore *wabi-sabi* is the beauty of things imperfect, impermanent, incomplete, modest, and, humble.

HAI

(Japanese) [HYE]

The smallest words can cause the greatest misunderstandings. *Hai* is a constant source of problems in East-West relations. The closest we have to it is an encouraging "ummm," combined with a sympathetic nod of the head. It means, "Yes, I am listening to you and I understand what you are saying." What it certainly doesn't mean is, "Yes, I agree with you." There lies the rub.

LÁNG XĪN GOU FÈI

(Mandarin) [LAHNG sheen GOH FAY]

Respect is still immensely important in China, and someone who does not pay respect to a person who helped him in the past may be said to have a "wolf heart and dog lungs." As you would expect of a civilization approximately 5,000 years old, Chinese uses a wide variety of wise sayings and proverbs as indirect insults and putdowns. Indeed, we have all seen stereotypes of the wise father quoting sayings at the rash or brash young son in films and TV series. Old Chinese sayings used small animals (like dogs, foxes, wolves, and cocks) to express insults. The wolf in sheep's clothing is exactly that in Chinese: *pi zhe yang pi de lang.*

GUANXI

(Mandarin) [GWAN-shee]

This is one of the essential ways of getting things done in traditional Chinese society. To build up good *guanxi*, you do things for others such as give them gifts, take them to dinner, or grant favors. Conversely, you can also "use up" your *guanxi* with someone by calling in favors owed. Once a favor is done, an unspoken obligation exists. Maybe because of this, people often try to refuse gifts because, sooner or later, they may have to repay the debt. However, the bond of *guanxi* is rarely acquitted, because once the relationship exists, it sets up an endless process that can last a lifetime.

MINGZHI

(Mandarin) [ming-DJIRR]

This term, based on the elements *ming*, meaning "dark, dim, otherworld," and *zhi*, meaning "paper," refers to "ghost money," which in parts of China is sold in bundles for ritual burnings for the dead. The Chinese burn *mingzhi* in metal containers at the side of the road, outside temples, businesses, and shops, or by street stalls. Printed on the money are the characters for "happiness," "peace," "good fortune," and so on, depending on what you wish to send to the gods, ghosts, or spirits. The burning of the money will ward off angry spirits or satisfy a "hungry ghost" from the underworld so it won't bother you or your family.

GAGUNG

(Cantonese) [ga-GUNG]

As a result of the one-child policy in China, the number of surplus males is now more than a hundred million. This sad term, which means "bare sticks" or "bare branches," refers to men who are unlikely to marry or to have families because of the skewed sex ratios.

GOTONG ROYONG

(Indonesian) [GOT-ong ROI-ongt]

Indonesians use *royong* to mean "mutual cooperation," or more precisely, the relationship between a group of people who are committed to accomplishing a task for mutual benefit. The word goes back to the days when small farmers worked together and used a common area in the center of the village or town for grazing their cattle.

The word is almost always used in conjunction with *gotong*, to form a phrase that means "to carry a heavy burden together," and it has been co-opted by politicians to convey the sense that the common good is more important than the individual.

OONT KIS KARWAT BAITHTA HAI

(Urdu) [UNT kiss KAHR-vat BYET-ta HYE]

This Urdu proverb, literally meaning "let us see which way the camel sits," is evocative of the desert region where camels are the main means of transportation. It is said that during a desert sandstorm you can always tell which direction the wind is blowing by the way that the camel sits. Of course, the clever camel always sits facing a direction that will protect its eyes and nostrils from the sand whipped up by the storm. Then the camel rider can take cover behind the camel's body. The closest that we get to the meaning in English is probably "let's see which way the wind blows."

MASALA CHAI

(Urdu) [ma–saH–lah tchye]

Chai in many languages is the term used for tea. It originates from the Chinese word for tea, *cha* (hence the British English colloquialism "Fancy a cup of char?"). Today, *chai* is a general term for a spiced milk tea that is sweetened, and the proper term for this spiced tea is *masala chai*, *masala* being an Indian word meaning any spiced blend. *Chai* is a beverage that is more popular in India than coffee is in the United States.

It is available on every street corner from vendors called *chai-valas*. These *chai-valas* carry pots of chai and serve it with lots of sugar in freshly fired earthen cups that are discarded after use. It is also a tradition in India to welcome guests with cups of *chai*. Each family has their own recipe and preparation method.

EURoPE

Germany throws its hat in the ring with the word *zusammenleben*, a more pragmatic notion of "getting along" in your family or in the community.

In a nice illustration of this *familismo*, the importance of families, David Bond, writing in *English Learning and Languages Review*, describes playing a game with an international group of friends, all living and working in a foreign country. The idea was for each member of the group to think up one word that for them summed up their faraway homeland. And what was the word that summed up his homeland for Bond himself? His spontaneous choice was the word "privacy," an almost diametrically opposed notion of "living together."

Europe is a continent now dedicated to the principle of "living together"—a plain and easily translatable notion, one would have thought. But in reality, the various takes on the idea of "living together" across European languages throw into relief the difficulties of translating an idea that may have hugely diverse implications in different cultures.

In Britain, for example, where an Englishman's home is his castle and it is possible to live for years without knowing his neighbors, the phrase "living together" refers without ambiguity to the domestic arrangement of unmarried couples. In Spain, the word *convivencia* alludes to "living together with others," the quality of a society where citizens get along by practicing tolerance and mutual respect. In this sense, it comes close to meaning a "civic culture."

ESPRIT DE L'ESCALIER

(French) [es-SPREE der less-KAL-iay]

A witty remark that occurs to you too late, literally on the way down the stairs. The *Oxford Dictionary of Quotations* defines *esprit de l'escalier* as "an untranslatable phrase, the meaning of which is that one only thinks on one's way downstairs of the smart retort one might have made in the drawing room."

FROUFROU

(French) [FROO-froo]

A rustling, especially that of a woman's skirt, and one of the nicest onomatopoeic words around. This lovely expression evokes the whole risqué world of *thés dansants, soirées intimes* (tea dances, intimate soirees), and the institution of the discreet venue, the *chambre séparée*. There is no way to imagine these delights other than in French.

SANS-CULOTTES

(French) [sonh-kyoo-LOT]

Literally "without breeches," this is the name given to a political movement that played a significant role in the French Revolution and in later social reform movements. The term refers to a disparate social group made up of artisans, storekeepers, and lower middle-class republicans who were united only in their hatred of the rich. The name came from the fact that the better-off members refused to wear breeches, which were associated with the aristocracy, and instead went about in pants (or trousers), the traditional dress of the working man.

RIRE JAUNE

(French) [reer JO-hne]

Literally, "to laugh yellowly," this expression is full of nuances that are hard to translate. As in other cultures, yellow is not a positive color in French, but *un jaune* doesn't mean "a coward" as in English, but rather "a traitor." In traditional medieval iconography, yellow is the color of Judas. To *rire jaune* is therefore to give a laugh that betrays your true feelings—an insincere laugh. It betrays you in trying to betray the other.

BOUDOIR

(French) [BOU-dwahr]

For a term now overlaid with so many carnal connotations, boudoir has innocent beginnings. Originally the dressing or sitting room next to a woman's bedroom, *boudoir* derives from the French *bouder*, which literally means "to pout" or "to sulk." A pouting room could be flirtatious; a sulking room seems to be a place where you send a misbehaving child; neither is the scene for seduction that a modern boudoir is thought to be.

TERROIR

(French) [TERR-wah]

One cannot speak of untranslatable French culture without a nod to viniculture, itself a profoundly mysterious business, full of nuances and shades. *Terroir*, Christina Waters tells us, is "what informs the bouquet and flavor notes of wines . . . a heady confluence of elements that taken together inform the final product." The term indicates the mixture of soil, climate, temperature, geographical location (e.g., longitude, latitude, altitude), possibly even lunar cycle, which express themselves in the finished product. Here culture and agriculture meet in the sensory signature of "a glass of wine." It could not be said more succinctly.

IL PÈTE PLUS HAUT QUE SON CUL

(French) [eel PET plew OH kuh sonh KEW]

A lovely image, but not a phrase necessarily to say directly to someone's face. It is rude and familiar and literally means "he's farting higher than his ass." Most often heard at work about a boss or colleague who has a very inflated opinion of him or herself, but you'd be careful not to be overheard and wouldn't necessarily use it around the office. It's more the sort of phrase that's dropped in over coffee, most definitely when the person described is not there. Also used to describe a friend that has become big-headed, or a stranger who is snooty and arrogant.

DOPPELGÄNGER

(German) [DOP-ple-GENG-er]

Literally a "double goer," the *Doppelgänger* of legend was one's ghostly shadow-self. This spooky creature lurked behind you and cast no reflection, and only you could see it. The English got hold of the word in the mid-nineteenth century and set about bastardizing it. Nowadays, it's more or less synonymous with "look-alike."

WELTSCHMERZ

(German) [VELT-shmairts]

A compound word consisting of *Welt* meaning "world" and *Schmerz* meaning "pain." Just as your head can hurt (*Kopfschmerzen*) or you can suffer from a stomachache (*Magenschmerzen*), so the world can hurt too. In its mildest form, this is "world-weariness." At the other extreme, it's an existential pain that leaves you reeling with a damaging, head-clutching despair.

SCHADENFREUDE

(German) [SHAH-den-FROI-der]

A compound word consisting of *Schaden* meaning "damage" and *Freude* meaning "joy." This is a dirty, cackle-rousing kind of happiness derived from someone else's misfortune. We're all disgustingly guilty of enjoying this emotion at some time or other.

DRACHENFUTTER

(German) [DRACH-en-FOOT-er]

Meaning "dragon fodder," this is the offering German husbands make to their wives—breathing raging fire at the cave entrance—when they've stayed out late or they have otherwise engaged in some kind of inappropriate behavior. A nice box of chocolates, or some flowers perhaps, to mask the beer fumes.

KORINTHENKACKER

(German) [KAW-rint-en-KAK-er]

A "raisin pooper"—that is, someone so taken up with life's trivial details that they spend all day crapping raisins. You can spot these types a mile off—it's that irritating pen pusher or filing fanatic whose favorite job is tidying up the stationery cupboard.

KRENTENKAKKER

(Dutch) [KREN-ten-kak-er]

Just so we don't mix up our languages, this is the same word as the German *Korinthenkacker*, but in Holland it means someone who doesn't like spending money. I'm afraid the equivalent to the German *Korinthenkacker* is expressed somewhat more graphically in Dutch as *mierenneuker*—"ant f–ker."

MET IEMAND IN DE KOFFER DUIKEN

(Dutch) [met ee-mahnt in duh KOF-er doy-kuh]

In the Netherlands you don't have a roll in the hay with someone, you "jump in a suitcase together"—possibly to elope, but probably suggesting a dirty weekend away. While not the kind of phrase you'd use to initiate a romantic encounter, this is still the sort of schoolyard/locker-room insult that will get a laugh from everyone, except perhaps the person on the receiving end.

UITWAAIEN

(Dutch) [OOT-vay-en]

A most useful and attractive verb meaning "to walk in the wind for fun." It conjures up a charming image of Dutch people outdoors, knowing just how to enjoy their landscape.

IT'S A DOG'S LIFE

(British English)

First mentioned in a sixteenth century manuscript, the expression was a nod toward the miserable conditions of a working dog's existence. But by the mid-seventeenth century, the meaning of the phrase had become completely opposite from its original connotations, having taken a turn from the proverb, "It's a dog's life, hunger and ease."

In the modern context, then, it represents a life of comfort—like the life of the beloved family dog who snoozes by the fire and symbolizes hearth and home.

BY HOOK OR BY CROOK

(British English)

It is good to find a phrase in common use that goes back as far as this one, and that appears (though this has not been conclusively proven) to connect the British to their feudal past. The first recorded use of the phrase is from the fourteenth century, when the peasantry were not allowed to cut down trees but were permitted to gather firewood from loose or dead branches that could be obtained using a hook (bill-hook) or a crook, a staff with a curved end like the kind shepherds would use. No doubt desperate peasants often exceeded the strict use of these tools, and so the term has evolved into its current usage meaning to achieve something by whatever means necessary.

BOB'S YOUR UNCLE

(British English)

A favorite British English expression whose origin is disputed. The most likely theory points to British Prime Minister Robert "Bob" Cecil appointing his nephew Chief Secretary for Ireland in 1887. Though he was unqualified, obtaining the position was easy enough when "Bob's your uncle." As such, the phrase refers to any task that may appear tricky but that can be accomplished quickly and simply once you know how, after which one can say with a flourish, "Bob's your uncle!"

HAIR OF THE DOG

(British English)

Across the Queen's green and pleasant land on any Sunday morning you can be sure that a large number of her loyal subjects are nursing a fierce headache after one beer too many the previous evening. British folk wisdom dictates that a shot of the drink that got you into this state will clear your head in no time. The phrase is thought to come from the ancient medical principle that like-cures-like: thus, a dog bite would be healed by rubbing it with a burned hair of the offending dog.

EVEN A WORM WILL TURN

(British English)

First recorded in English in a 1546 collection of proverbs by John Heywood, it is a proverbial phrase to acknowledge that even a mild and lowly being is capable of defending itself if pushed. Shakespeare also employed the phrase in the play *Henry V*:

*The smallest worm will turn, being trodden on
And doves will peck in safeguard of their brood.*

COCK AND BULL STORY

(British English)

A fanciful, rambling tale that cannot be believed. Robert Burton's *The Anatomy of Melancholy* (1621) cites the first English use of this phrase: "Some men's whole delight is to talk of a Cock and Bull over a pot." The Buckinghamshire market town of Stony Stratford, which in its day was a crucial coach stop between London and the north of England, claims that the phrase originates from the exaggerated stories by owners (or travelers) of the rival pubs—one called the The Cock and one called The Bull. However, this in itself probably qualifies as a cock and bull story; the real origins are obscure but may have derived from the seventeenth century French term *coq-a-l'âne*, meaning "from rooster to donkey."

CAVOLI RISCALDATI

(Italian) [KAH-voh-lee ree-skahl-DAH-tee]

Literally "reheated cabbage," this Italian phrase describes a pointless attempt to revive a former love affair, and comes from a proverb: *cavoli riscaldati né amore ritornato non fu mai buono*—"neither reheated cabbage nor revived love is ever any good."

A OUTRA METADE
DA LARANJA

(Portuguese) [ah OH-trah mi-TAH-dee
dah lah-RANH-zhah]

The phrase *a outra metade da laranja* is another way to say "my
better half" in Portuguese. Its literal translation is "the other half
of the orange," implying that only with your partner do you make
a whole. Portugal has long been associated with the growth and
export of oranges. Persian *narang* and Arabic *naranj* show the history
of the word, which originated in India with the Sanskrit *naranga*
and was brought to Western Europe by the Arabs when they
conquered Spain; Greek *portokali* and Turkish *portakal* show the
association with Portugal.

MAGARI

(Italian) [mag-AH-ree]

A rich and positive word with multiple uses and sprinkled everywhere in conversation. It is strongly evocative of the ebullient Italian spirit, meaning anything from "even if" to "Rather!" or "You bet!" It has a wonderfully affirmative value, even when expressing no more than a fervent wish such as *magari fosse vero!* —"If only it were true!"

ATTACCABOTTONE

(Italian) [at-TAK-ka-bot-OWN-eh]

This is a bore who "buttonholes" you and tells you long tales of woe. You long to escape from an *attaccabottone*, but somehow it's always difficult to get away.

SAUDADE

(Portuguese) [sow-DAH-dee]

Saudade is a kind of intense nostalgia that only the Portuguese people are supposed to feel or understand. According to Katherine Vaz, who titled her 1994 novel Saudade, it is "yearning so intense for those who are missing, or for vanished times or places, that absence is the most profound presence in one's life. A state of being, rather than merely a sentiment." It can also refer to a yearning for a lost lover.

PASEO

(Spanish) [pass-EH-o]

The time of evening when the heat of the sun is diminishing and the siesta is over is the moment of the paseo. It is the time when the Spanish dress themselves and their children up to the nines and go out to walk around the main square, or up and down the shady avenues. It's a time of meeting and looking, seeing and being seen. Late on summer nights, after the cena, the same gentle ambling takes place until well after midnight, with small children often dozing on their parents' shoulders.

PÍCARO

(Spanish) [PEE-ka-ro]

This word has wide and colorful associations. Students of Spanish literature come across *la picaresca* as a style of novel, a kind of episodic storywriting usually involving rogues drifting through society of the kind well-illustrated by Cervantes' *Don Quixote*. The typical *pícaro* is one who lives off his wits in order to survive.

La picaresca summons up a whole tapestry of human life at its most inventive, ingenious, and resilient. *Pícaro* can mean smart, astute, clever, cunning, mischievous, naughty, shameless, wicked, saucy, impudent, lustful, roguish, dishonorable, bold, daring, racy, brazen, or cheeky. It practically sums up the human condition!

NAROBIC BIGOSU

(Polish) [na–RO–beetch bee–GO–soo]

The expression *narobic bigosu* means "to make a mess" or cause problems or confusion. It comes from the noun *bigos*, which is a popular Polish dish made with sauerkraut, sausage, and mushrooms as the basic ingredients. You then add whatever else you have in the cupboard to the stew.

Just so we are clear, if you are setting out to tell someone you're making *bigos* for supper, this is expressed as *zrobi bigos*.

YOLKI-PALKI

(Russian) [YAWL-kee-PAHL-kee]

A peculiar Russian expression that could express surprise, dismay, or pleasure, depending on the situation. The phrase literally translates as "fir trees and sticks" but is probably approximated in English by the expression "Holy cow!"

LÍTOST

(Czech) [LEE-tost]

This is an untranslatable emotion that only a Czech person would suffer from, defined by Milan Kundera as "a state of torment created by the sudden sight of one's own misery." Devices for coping with extreme stress, suffering, and change are often special and unique to cultures and born out of the meeting of despair with a keen sense of survival.

NIE DLA WSZYSTKICH SKRZYPCE GRAJA

(Polish) [nieh dla FSHIST-keech SKSHIP-tseh GRA-yonh]

This Polish proverb translates literally into English as "the violin doesn't play for everybody." The Polish word for violin is *skrzypce* and this word derives from the word *skrzyp*, which means "creak" or "groan." While there is no common translation or equivalent in English, we all know the horrible ear-splitting screeching and scratchiness of a violin in the hands of a novice. Next time you see a person attempting a task for which they quite obviously lack the required skill, you could obliquely drop an observation that "the violin doesn't play for everybody."

POSHLOST

(Russian) [PAWSH-lerst]

This word, which one can imagine uttered with a contemptuous curl of the lip, indicates an acute awareness of the hollowness of false values and the need to deride and deflate them. The Russian writer Vladimir Nabokov devoted many pages to a damning commentary on *poshlost*, which he claimed to have fought against all his life. He describes *poshlost* as "cheap, sham, common, pink-and-blue, in bad taste." Russian dictionaries also offer fairly negative definitions such as "spiritually and morally base, petty, worthless, mediocre" and "commonplace . . . devoid of higher interests and needs."

RAZLIUBIT

(Russian) [raz-lyoo-BEET]

This melancholic, bittersweet word is used to describe falling out of love. Specifically, it's losing a feeling for someone one once loved but no longer feel the same way about. It's a brilliantly succinct word and captures that feeling of the maddeningly ephemeral nature of love.

MEGILLAH

(Yiddish) [meh-GILL-a]

From the Hebrew word for "scroll," the *megillah*, or the Biblical book of Esther, is read out on the Jewish festival of Purim. In colloquial speech, it is a versatile term covering anything long, complicated, dull, or unnecessarily dragged out. "Don't give me a *megillah*" means "spare me the details." In recent years, it's also come to mean a major event or cause for excitement.

BUPKIS

(Yiddish) [BUP-kiss]

This word, literally meaning "beans," has come to mean "nothing" or "something that is worthess." It is generally spoken in disgust or despair, and "I haven't got *bupkis*" relates to the English phrase, "I haven't got a bean," or "nothing but a hill of beans."

CHUTZPAH

(Yiddish) [CHUTS-pa]

This word roughly translates as a kind of presumption layered with arrogance, although that would deny the underlying humor of the term. You can't say this word without appreciating its gutsiness. It is audacity without shame and, provided the mix is more spunk than impudence, not necessarily an undesirable quality. To wheel out the old cliché, *chutzpah* is best summed up by the boy who kills his parents and then pleads for mercy from the judge—on grounds that he's an orphan.

SCHMUCK

(Yiddish) [SHMUK]

From the German for "ornament," this is a surprisingly innocent derivation, considering that it has come to mean "penis." Not a word to be uttered lightly, and certainly not in polite company. However, used discerningly in the right circumstances, it has considerable force as an insult.

LUFTMENSCH

(Yiddish) [LUFT-mensh]

Literally this translates as "one who lives on air." You get the idea. There is usually one of these in every family—an impractical person who is overly dependent on the family for survival.

THE FAR NORTH

Residents of Nordic countries are unlike any other people in the world. Thomas Hylland Eriksen writes, "Foreign stereotypes tend to depict Scandinavians as wealthy, enlightened, rational, and bored Protestants with strong welfare states, lax rules of sexual morality, and an institutionalized yearning for nature and simplicity." But there are significant differences between the nationalities for those who can see them. Eriksen quotes the following example:

A Swede, a Dane, and a Norwegian are shipwrecked on the proverbial desert island. A genie appears out of thin air, informing them that they can each have a wish granted. The Swede immediately says, "I want to go home to my large and comfortable bungalow with the Volvo, video, and slick IKEA furniture." So he vanishes. The Dane then says, "I want to go back to my cozy little flat in Copenhagen, to sit on my soft sofa, feet on the table, next to my sexy girlfriend, with a six-pack of lagers." Off he flies. The Norwegian, after giving the problem a bit of thought, then tells the the genie, "Gee, I suddenly feel so terribly lonely here, so I guess I wish for my two friends to come back."

Denmark, of course, is where both Swedes and Norwegians go to enjoy themselves in the land of *hygge*. The *Copenhagen Post* reported, "No single aspect of Danish culture has baffled foreigners more. A near-untranslatable concept incorporating elements of English coziness, Norwegian *koselighet*, Finnish *vilhtylisyys*, French *douillet*, Dutch *gezelligheid*, and Irish *craic*." Ah, that's clearer now.

The Finns have made a virtue of their perpetual cold by insulating themselves in saunas, and enjoy a custom known as *löyly*, that incredible heat wave that engulfs you when you throw water on the hot stove. All very purifying and healthy for a nation whose language enjoys a surfeit of vowels.

What then unites these nations and cultures? *Folkelighed* or *folklighet*, depending on where you are, is a central concept throughout the fundamentally anti-elitist Scandinavian culture. United, but in friendly tension, the Nordic countries represent a wonderland of untranslatable customs, beliefs, and nuances of social behavior.

HYGGE

(Danish) [HUE-gah]

Hygge comes from the Norwegian word for "well-being" and is often translated as "coziness." Yet it is in fact much more than this. Grammatically used as an adjective, verb, and noun, it describes the feeling of well-being that comes from the simple pleasures of life at home. It can refer to enjoying time with friends or relaxing with family. It means warm sweaters on cold evenings, contented quiet days at home, eating dinner by candlelight. At its heart, it is that warm homey glow that comes from enjoying the little things in life.

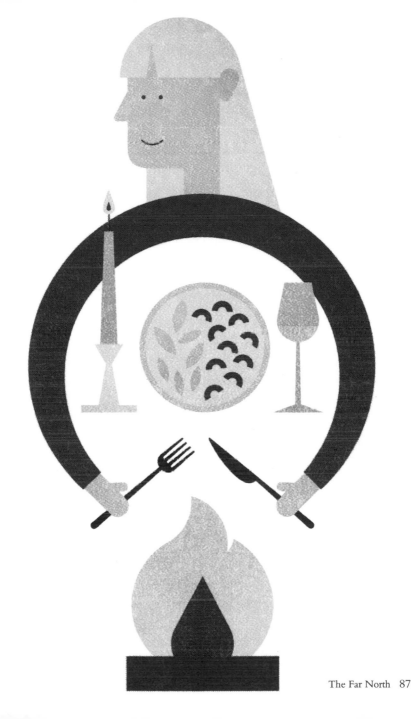

SMÖRGÅS

(Swedish) [SMERR-goss]

The world-famous Scandinavian open sandwich, also known as *smørrebrød* (Danish) and *smørbrød* (Norwegian). But isn't an open sandwich just a closed one that has been ceremonially prized open like a reluctant clam or a mummy's tomb? No indeed, for to cover the top of an open sandwich would be to abuse the filling, or rather the topping. It would deface the trimmings and humiliate the emancipated pink shrimp that grace it, lying there in all their naked glory, parading themselves and basking amid a shallow sea of fresh watercress, luring potential diners to sample their wares. We should be wary of contaminating this concept by association with the common and rather plain sandwich of middle-class picnics.

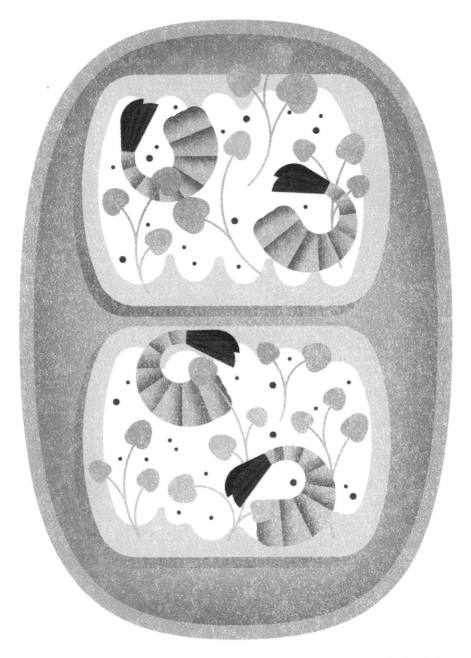

NIDSTANG

(Norwegian) [NID-stang]

A runic cursing pole used by the Vikings as a way of bringing destruction and disturbance to their enemies. These long poles were carved with insults and curses, and ceremonies were performed to activate their destructive magic. The pole was intended to disrupt and anger the *landvaettir*, or "earth spirits," living in the ground beneath the enemy's house. Believe it or not, there are those even today who continue this tradition.

SAGA

(Icelandic) [SAH-gah]

A long story of heroic achievement, especially a medieval prose narrative in Old Norse or Old Icelandic. It has also come to mean a long, involved, rambling, seemingly never-ending account or tales of incidents. Literally, it means "narrative."

LAGOM

(Swedish) [lag-OHM]

The Swedish culture could be summarized in the word *lagom*. It references an undefined state between extremes, such as "not too much, not too little," or "just right." It can refer to the temperature of a warm bath, or the correct fit of a jacket. But these translations do not fully capture the true meaning of the word. Swedish commentator Dr. Bengt Gustavsson argued that the *lagom* mentality can be seen as the trait that gives Swedish society its characteristic stability and yet an openness to external influences. The word alludes to the avoidance of both conspicuous success and humiliating failure, which is deeply ingrained in the Swedish psyche. It is the inclination among Swedes to shun ostentation, accept modest rewards, and be good team players.

RETKAHTAA

(Finnish) [REHT-kahkh-tah]

In English, we talk about being drunk with love; the Finnish use the word *retkahtaa* to mean both falling in love and falling off the wagon. Literally meaning to "fall down forcefully and unintentionally," it also conveys the suddenness and shock that falling in love can be to some.

BEJAKA

(Swedish) [bay-AH-kah]

A word that frequently recurs in Swedish and is quite untranslatable outside the Scandinavian and Germanic languages, it encapsulates a whole philosophy. *Livsbejakelse* consists of *liv*, meaning "life," and *bejakelse*, meaning "saying yes," hence "affirmation of life." *Bejaka* means an enthusiastic, optimistic, or joyful attitude, and, when applied to life, signifies far more than just agreeing to live. Within this one word we sense a greeting—a welcome to all the vicissitudes that life may bring and an understanding acceptance of people and things as they are.

UTEPILS

(Norwegian) [OOT-er-pillss]

You have to live through the long dark months of a Norwegian winter to appreciate the annual Norwegian rite of *utepils*. Literally it means "the first drink of the year taken out of doors." Easter is barely past, with its tradition of *hyttepåske*—your Easter visit to your remote cabin—and the days are at last getting longer. Although it's still practically freezing, everyone is lining up to invite you to a first *utepils* get-together at a favorite bar.

HANKIKANTO

(Finnish) [HON-ki-kon-toh]

This is a typical Finnish word that resists translation into many languages. *Hankikanto* is a frozen crust on the surface of snow that is strong enough to walk on. This matters to anyone planning a long winter trek, because snow conditions affect the choice of route and equipment.

ÁLFREKA

(Icelandic) [OHL-fray-kah]

Appreciation of elves in Iceland is a serious business, according to Nigel Pennick, writer on spiritual traditions. One of the very worst Norse curses that can be invoked is the *álfreka*, literally, the "driving away of the elves" or the earth spirits from a place, which leaves the ground spiritually dead.

THE ANCIENT WORLD

It is impossible to speak English without speaking Greek, as Dr. John Kalaras demonstrates in the following paragraph from *The Genesis of Classical Drama*, composed entirely of words of Greek origin:

> The prologue, the theme and the epilogue comprised the trilogy of drama while synthesis, analysis, and synopsis characterized the phraseology of the text. The syntax and phraseology used by scholars, academicians, and philosophers in their rhetoric had many grammatical idioms and idiosyncrasies.

Our intellectual debt to Greek is without question. A nicely untranslatable example of what linguists call "a rhetorical device" is the word *accismus*, from the Greek *akkismos*, meaning "coyness" or "affectation." This refers to how we may refuse something in a slightly dramatic way to show that we would actually like to have it. "Oh, no, I couldn't possibly take the last piece, delicious as it was . . . and my favorite dessert as well. No, I simply couldn't. Well . . . "

The ancient Greeks not only had many ideas and concepts that were quite particular to them and challenging to translate into modern terms, but also a long tradition of uniquely Greek feelings.

The Romans, in their turn, gave us town planning, sophisticated techniques of construction, military organization, and, in due course, the European interlanguage of Vulgar or Medieval Latin, carried by the Christian church on the back of their empire.

Linguistically speaking, at the root of all these great traditions stands the legendary pre-Christian civilization of ancient India, with its profound culture explored and expressed through the medium of Sanskrit, and subsequently distributed all over Europe and Asia Minor. All the Indo European family of tongues owe their origin to Sanskrit and its civilization.

EIDOLON

(Greek) [AY-doh-lon]

This term in Greek thought, meaning something like "image of a person" or "empty shadow," was what descended into Hades after death as a shade or ghost. It did not indicate survival of an "immortal soul" in the sense that Western thought later aassumed. As we see from Homer's epic *The Odyssey* and other accounts of visiting Hades, the departed were literally "shadows of their former selves." The Greeks believed that two vital elements of the human being were lost at the point of death—one was *thymos*, the active, willed element of the human being. The other was the life principle or something like consciousness, known as *psyche*. Following death, this became a mere *eidolon*. The idea of *eidolon* explained for the Greeks why we sometimes see dead people in dreams or in dreamlike states. It has continued its meaning in the modern word "idol" with the same suggestion of "hollow image."

IN FLAGRANTE

(Latin) [in flag-RANT-ay]

This word literally means "while the thing is blazing," but basically means that you are caught in the act of whatever you are doing. When a person is arrested *in flagrante delicto* the only evidence that is needed to convict him or her is to prove that fact. When someone is caught *in flagrante seducto* they have been caught with their underpants down.

REALIA

(Latin) [ray-AH-lee-ah]

The word realia has its origins in Latin, but not the language spoken by the classical Romans, rather the medieval language of education, science, and philosophy. *Realia* means "real things," as opposed to words, which are neither "things" nor "real." Therefore it refers to objects and so requires the teacher or educator to put genuine articles or examples of things in front of a pupil, rather than simply to refer to them by using terms of vocabulary.

KHAOS

(Greek) [CHA-os]

This resonant word has come down to us via Latin as "chaos," but this represents only one aspect of its original meaning. In Greek mythology, as recorded by Hesiod, creation in the form of three gods arose out of the void known as Khaos, which was itself a primordial godhead. Therefore, the term *khaos* meant a universe where there was nothing formed—a state of yawning nothingness, empty and hollow. The name comes from the Greek verb stem *kha-*, meaning "to yawn" or "gape."

SUB ROSA

(Latin) [sub ROH-zah]

Literally "under the rose," a lovely phrase with a long history. It is supposed to come from the gift of a rose, recorded in Greek and Roman myth, which Cupid made to the god of silence in return for keeping quiet about his mother Venus's many amours. Over time this gave rise to the practice of hanging a rose at meetings to indicate confidentiality, thus sub rosa, "under the rose." The rose became a feature of the central boss of vaulted chambers such as, for instance, a monastic chapter room where the community met, and was also placed over the confessional. In private houses, too, from Roman times onward, a decorative rose in the plasterwork of a dining-room ceiling indicated an assurance to guests of their host's discretion.

QUALIA

(Latin) [KWAH-lee-ah]

This word's meaning could not be more opposed to *realia*. In philosophical jargon, *qualia* are those experiences that we cannot possibly describe in words, such as seeing a specific color. Whatever science says about colors being no more than reflected wavelengths in the light spectrum, try declaring that about a sunset or a red-light district and see the looks you get. Red is red is red, and therefore falls into the category of so-called *qualia*.

CAILLEACH

(Gaelic) [KAL-yach]

This derives from *caille*, meaning "a veil," and originally meant "a nun," but came also to mean "an old woman" or "hag." However, in English this term is now corrupted with associations of witchcraft or supernatural and malign activity. In Celtic mythology, the *cailleach* is considered the "crone" aspect of the Triple Goddess. In a telling metaphor, the cruel winds of early April, punishing the first green shoots of the year, are seen as the work of a wild cailleach or storm goddess who wields her switch against the young plants until finally giving up in disgust and disappearing for another season. Similarly, around Halloween, the *cailleach* appears as the winter goddess bringing the first frosts. She is one who needs to be appeased. Traditionally, the first farmer to finish harvesting would make a corn-dolly or *cailleach* from the straw and pass it on to the next and so on until it came to the last farmer. This farmer was obliged to keep an eye on the "old woman" until the next year's harvest.

THA GRÀDH AGAM ORT

(Scots Gaelic) [hah GRAHGH aguhm ort]

This is literally "I have love on you," which sounds almost as if you have accidentally spilled your love over someone and are now apologizing for getting love on their new shirt. An even more intimate way to say "I love you" is *tha gaol mo chridhe agam ort-sa*, which is literally "I love you with all my heart."

GOISEAR

(Scots Gaelic) [GO-sherr]

This word has entered modern Scottish English as "guiser" and now refers to children going door-to-door at Halloween and Christmas time. But in the old tradition, the *goisearan* were present at all the great festivals of the year and were a band of village youths dressed up with masked faces as kings, queens, bishops, and nuns. Making as much noise as possible, they brought blessings to every house in exchange for presents. Traditionally, these offerings were carried off in a lambskin bag known as *uilim* to a barn where the revelers then held a large feast and a dance and invited their girlfriends.

BRÀC

(Scots Gaelic) [BRAHK]

A deer, but also with wonderful evocation. According to context it can be the roar of a stag, the curve of an antler, or the curve of a wave immediately before breaking.

NIRVANA

(Sanskrit) [neer-VAH-nah]

In Buddhism, this is a state of perfect happiness. It is the ineffable ultimate where one has attained disinterested wisdom and compassion. A transcendent state in which there is no suffering, desire, or sense of self and the subject is released from the effects of karma. It represents the final goal in Buddhism. Originally from the Sanskrit *nirva*, "be extinguished," *nis*, "out," and *va*, "to blow."

YOGA

(Sanskrit) [YOH-gah]

Meaning "union," it refers to the union of the mind, body, and spirit. This is a Hindu spiritual and ascetic discipline that includes breath control, simple meditation, and the adoption of specific body postures widely practiced for relaxation.

MANTRA

(Sanskrit) [MAN-trah]

Generally known as a combination of syllables for meditation or affirmations often found on mani wheels, one of the oldest and best known *mantras* is the *om mane pad me hum* of yogic chanting. But *mantra* in Sanskrit also has a deeper and more powerful meaning. *Man-* means "mental" or "in mind," and *-tra* stands for a tool. So the word represents a verbal instrument for mental imagery, a non-linguistic expression of the mind.

FARTHER AFIELD

Anthropologists have long found refreshment and inspiration in the purity and simplicity of so-called "primitive cultures." Nearly all indigenous cultures retain a spiritual awareness and respect for the natural world on which they depend for their survival. The surrounding environment is often seen as an appearance of a deeper interconnected reality in which humans and animals, plants, birds, and trees are all soul-fellows. Systems of worship and belief accompany these insights.

Anthropologist Carlos Castaneda related a challenging account of his apprenticeship in Mexico with Don Juan, the Yaqui shaman. For good or ill, the shaman has access to powerful forces underlying all nature. Don Juan speaks of the *nagual*, the invisible reality that lies behind all creation. "The *nagual* is the part of us for which there is no description—no words, no names, no feelings, no knowledge."

Commentators use terms like "unspeakable" and "indescribable" for the *nagual*. Untranslatable? It would seem so.

R. M. W. Dixon in *The Languages of Australia* discusses the Indigenous Australian Yidiny dialect and its sensitivity to different kinds of noise. These include *dalmba*, the sound of cutting; *maral*, the noise of hands being clapped together; *nyurrugu*, the noise of talking heard a long way off when the words cannot quite be made out; and *yuyurngal*, the noise of a snake sliding through the grass.

Here are some other words that help us get a glimpse at a culture behind the translation.

BILLABONG

(Indigenous Australian) [BILL-er-bong]

This word is an Indigenous Australian term that has passed into common usage in Australia but is quite untranslatable when out of context of the landscape. It is literally "a branch of a river cut off from the main stream." The term is well known due to the pseudo-Australian national anthem and poem by Banjo Paterson, dating from the 1890s, *Waltzing Matilda*. This song is brimming with untranslatables:

Oh there once was a swagman camped in the billabong
Under the shade of a Coolibah tree
And he sang as he looked at the old billy boiling
Who'll come a-waltzing Matilda with me.

KŌHANGA REO

(Maori) [koh-hang-ah RAY-oh]

Many indigenous languages face extinction, particularly in places that are less isolated from the world and where the people of the language group are a minority group dying without passing on their knowledge. This is true of languages in places like Australia, North America, Canada, and New Zealand. *Kōhanga reo* is the Maori effort to stop this from happening to their language. Literally translating as "language nest," this word refers to Maori-speaking preschools, where the language is actively being taught. Now more than 50 percent of the Maori speakers are under twenty-five years old.

BOL

(Mayan) [BOWL]

There's nothing like telling things as they are—the Mayans of south Mexico and Honduras use the word *bol* for in-laws as well as stupidity. Also, not very flatteringly, the root word for *bol* indicates a dazed befuddlement or stupor. Some things are universal and it seems that most cultures find it hard to cope with the in-laws.

HOZH'Q

(Navajo) [HOE-shk]

This means "the beauty of life, as seen and created by a person." For the Navajo, this is something that grows from within a human being and spreads outward to permeate the universe. It can be intellectual, emotional, moral, aesthetic, and biological. Navajo life and culture are very much based on this concept of *hozh'q*, and indeed the goal of life is the unity of experience. *Hozh'q* expresses ideas of order, happiness, health, and well-being, as well as balance and harmony. Hence, it is not only a way of looking at life, but a way to live.

POWWOW

(Algonquin) [POW-wow]

This word originally referred only to a gathering of medicine men, coming together to perform a healing ceremony. Now it has come to mean a gathering of any kind of people and evokes an idea of talking and celebrating.

KANGA

(Swahili) [KAHN-ga]

The *kanga* is the traditional printed cloth worn by women that is encoded with a proverb or message. They are worn in pairs, one is often worn over a dress or a skirt to protect the clothing underneath, and the other might be worn as a head covering or tied as a sling to carry a baby. Women can speak volumes to the community without saying a word. *Kanga* proverbs include *mdhaniaye ndiye kumbe siye*, literally translating as "the one whom you think is the right one is the wrong one," in other words, "you are barking up the wrong tree"; *moyo wangu Sultani, cha mtu sikitamani*, literally, "my heart is like Sultan, I don't long for anybody else's property," or, "I am satisfied"; and *siku ya kufa nyani miti yote huteleza*, "the day a monkey is destined to die, all trees get slippery," or, "there is no escaping one's fate."

BADO

(Swahili) [BAH-doh]

This word appears to translate quite transparently, as one of the first a child comes to understand and make use of, the word that parents learn to dread because they hear it so much: "no!" However, *bado* has a deeper meaning and is actually used to say "no" when it is theoretically possible that the action may occur in the future. Employed to answer questions such as "Will you buy a new car?" or "Do you have children?" it means "No, not yet." Another Swahili phrase *sasa hivi* translates literally as "soon" or "right away," but be careful as "just now" might mean several hours in the future to the South African speaking with you.

UBUNTU

(Bantu) [uu-BOON-tuu]

From the Zulu phrase "*Umuntu ngumuntu ngabantu*," which literally means that a person is a person only through other people. *Ubuntu* has its roots in humanist African philosophy, where the idea of community is one of the building blocks of society. *Ubuntu* is that untranslatable concept of a common humanity, as popularized by Desmond Tutu.

BACHEQUE

(Lingala) [bah-CHECK]

This word describes the local "man on the street," the one who lives on nothing but his wits. The closest English translation might be "con artist." This is the man about Kinshasa who will sell you a car (especially when yours has mysteriously disappeared the day before), organize a night out on the town for you, or a tour of the local sights. Wearing a loud shirt and the best designer watch, *bacheque* serve a vital brokering purpose when the formal economy has dramatically broken down. They change currency, establish market prices, and give the capital its characteristic feel.

PALATYI

(Bantu) [pa-LA-tee-yeh]

The West African Bantu people talk of a supernatural being thought to haunt their land. It's called the *palatyi*, or "plat-eye prowl," and is a mythical animal-like ghost that comes and scratches on your door on cold, dark nights. What could possibly be more frightening if you live in a remote village and you hear something in the night?

WORD FINDER

Christopher J. Moore is an author, translator, and editor of both adult and children's books; he is the author of *In Other Words* (2004) and *How to Speak Brit* (2014). He holds degrees in modern languages and applied linguistics from the universities of Oxford and Edinburgh.

Lan Truong is an illustrator based in Portland, Oregon. Her work is influenced by vintage matchbox labels and posters.

Simon Winchester is a British journalist and bestselling author of numerous works of nonfiction, notably *The Surgeon of Crowthorne* (1998) and *The Men who United the States* (2014). His career has sent him around the globe and he now lives in New York and Massachusetts.